SUICIDE PSYCHOLOGY

CONNOR WHITELEY

DEDICATION

Thank you to all my readers without you I couldn't do
what I love.

INTRODUCTION

There is no easy way to talk about suicide and there are even fewer books on the topic.

In our society, it is almost a dirty word, a taboo topic and something that mustn't be addressed at all costs.

Not only are these societal and personal attitudes outrageous, wrong and disgusting, but they aren't helpful. As well as they create so many powerful myths and misconceptions that end up making suicide worse, and these myths kill people.

Whilst I fully admit this book tackles a difficult topic, it is actually written slightly differently to the rest of my psychology books. And this book is completely fact and evidence-based, but there are a lot of pieces of unofficially advice and tips in the book.

As well as in a way, this book is really written in a great, easy-to-understand way that's engaging and conversational (like all my books) for three different groups of people. But given how interconnected everyone actually is when it comes to suicide, everyone benefits from everything in this book.

Therefore, the vast majority of readers will undoubtedly be my normal audience of psychology students and professionals that want to deepen their knowledge of this topic.

As a result, this book covers so many amazing topics from myths about suicide to the risk factors and mental health to more nuanced topics like suicides amongst children, teenagers and young people.

In addition, maybe you suffered a recent loss to suicide and you're confused, worried and maybe feel a bit of guilt about it. This book helps you to understand that this is normal, it wasn't your fault and it helps to explain what actually could have happened to your loved one.

One of the entire points of this book is to help explain to everyone how suicide really works because most people just work off the awfully harming myths that are wrong. This book is designed and written to help people become more aware, learn what happened to their loved one and something else entirely.

In the case that someone is suicidal is reading this book, then of course get professional help **immediately**. But in case that seems too impossible right now, this helps to explain what's going on, how to talk to other people about what you're experiencing and why it is critical you get help immediately.

Personally, this entire book and every single word in it, is meant to help you as the reader. It is meant to help you learn more, become more aware and it might even save a life.

I don't know if this book will but I wrote it with the intention that I could save a life and help people.

Therefore, if you want a great, easy-to-understand book that has tons of references and research behind it (including the reference list at the end) that's written in a helpful, conversational and engaging tone then definitely buy this book.

And normally in these introductions, I introduce myself at a bit of length, but I don't want to keep you away from learning more about this critical and fascinating area.

Therefore, all I'll quickly say is I'm Connor Whiteley, an author of over 30 psychology books, a psychology student from the University of Kent, England and the host of The Psychology World Podcast available on all major podcast apps and YouTube with over 185 episodes looking at a wide range of psychology topics.

Now we know a bit more about each other, let's dive into this interesting, slightly tragic and fascinating area of psychology.

MALE SUICIDES: A SILENT CRISIS

For the first chapter of the book, I really wanted to start off with a sort of introductory chapter that looked at why suicide is such a critical topic to focus on. That's why this first chapter and some chapters after chapter three are drawn from podcast episodes of The Psychology World Podcast as this will help you to see my own journey of easing into this difficult topic before deciding to write this book.

Enjoy.

***

Male Suicides: A Silent Clinical Psychology Crisis

After wanting to do a psychology podcast episode for a while on suicide, I've finally felt like I'm ready to do one because this is a difficult topic for anyone, some more than others. Because no one wants to talk about suicide and I understand it because it is a "dark" topic. But that creates problems because people experiencing suicide ideation, don't feel like they can talk to anyone about it.

Therefore, the aim of this episode is to help shine some light on the psychology of suicide so we can all become more aware.

Male Suicides:

In the USA around 35,000 men commit suicide each year because of various factors and some of these we will look at today. In other words, in the USA that means 1 man kills themselves every 15 minutes.

In Canada, around 3,000 men die each year by suicide, over 50 men each week.

Also I know I'm only talking about men here and that's because in the USA 75% of suicides are done by men.

In addition the most concerning thing about this is that these rates are rising because the US Centers for Disease Control report found that suicide rates had increased by around 2% from 2006 to 2017. As well as this might not sound like a lot but it's actually a 26 percent increase from 1999.

Therefore, I just want to stop for a moment and… say how scary this is. Personally this scares me that so many men (and women) feel the need to commit suicide because their life has gotten so bad and they don't feel like they have any other option.

Additionally, I know a lot of people who have never experienced suicidal ideation can't fully understand it, and some even just call these people attention seekers. (That's outrageous) But as humans we are hard-wired to survive, live and pass on. What

I'm trying to say here is no one *wants* to commit suicide for no reason.

These people feel like they *have* to commit suicide.

Inadequate Suicide Prevention Measures:

Before I talk about the next section, I want to mention that I am not discrediting, attacking or "slating" current suicide prevention services, what I am doing is commenting on them from a book called *Men's Issues and Men's Mental Health* by Springer that the book points out are core arguments about the existing approaches.

Also as I've mentioned on the podcast before, in psychology I love how we're always critically thinking so we can improve services so we can help people and make their lives better.

The first argument the book makes is about the narrow focus on the concept of masculinity and how it lacks any peripheral vision to look at the adverse social context experienced by many men.

Personally, I have always said this and this point extends into societal factors as a whole. Since traditionally men are meant to be strong, emotionless people who get on with male jobs, and they leave the women to be the emotional wrecks that society depicts them as.

This traditional view of men is useless, extremely unhelpful and it is a major factor in male mental health, because of this societal view men don't want to come forward and get professional help. Due to getting professional help makes them look less manly, weak, pathetic and all that other rubbish that society thinks about men who want to better their lives.

Therefore, this traditional view of men does need to change.

Blaming, Shaming and Male Deficits:

This is another great point to make about suicides and this can be taken in two parts.

The first can be broadened to all suicides there is a blame and shame culture around suicide because I've heard of tons of comments from people from all walks of life blaming the person who committed suicide for their actions. But I want to come back to an earlier point because no one wants to kill themselves, there are factors in their life (both genetic and environmental) that make them feel like they have no other option.

So the fact that instead of looking at their life and blaming those factors, people feel the need to blame the person who killed themselves because they felt they had no other option.

This is just... sad, outrageous and awful that as a society we feel like it's okay to do that.

In addition, it is possible that this is one reason why people don't speak out that they're experiencing suicidal ideation because they don't want to be blamed for how they're feeling. As well as I mention this in different forms in various mental health episodes of the Podcast.

This is sadly nothing new.

However, on the flip side, there's blaming male mental health on alleged male deficits. For example, males are typically stubborn. I know some men are, but that is no excuse not to help people or not take their mental health seriously.

Male Friendly Services

Now this is an argument I've adopted from the references below because the friendliness of a mental health services towards a group of people is always a problem in clinical psychology, and this is where the problem with the lack of diversity within clinical psychology really shows itself.

Therefore, I want to hammer it home again because with the lack of male clinical psychologists from different backgrounds. It means that there aren't that many relatable people that men can have therapy with and build a therapeutic alliance.

Since men might not want to talk about their difficulties in front of a woman because they may believe they shouldn't look "weak" in front of the fairer sex. This is where a male therapist who they can relate with could be useful.

Conclusion:

Originally, I was going to go on to talk about more the nitty-gritty findings of suicides in men but I'll save that for another podcast episode.

Yet I do want to finish up by saying if you or someone you love is complementing suicide, please, please, please seek immediate help.

In the UK, you can contact *Samaritans* and *Mind*.

In the US, you can **use the 24/7 contact service at** the National Suicide Prevention Lifeline**, 1-800-273-TALK, or reach out to the Crisis Text Line by texting TALK to 741741.**

If you're in a different country, please find your country's equivalent and get help.

MYTHS ABOUT SUICIDE

The reason why this is the second chapter in the book is simply because I want to tackle a lot of utterly stupid myths right now, just so we can get them out of the way and we can focus on facts.

Personally, I hate these myths with an utter passion because they are harmful, evil and just end up causing a lot more damage to people.

And the entire point of this book is to help raise awareness and maybe help people too.

To that end this chapter will look at 12 myths in varying amounts of detail just so moving forward we are all on the same page, and we can all interpret this information without seeing it through any myths.

As well as whilst I am extremely passionate about this area, I do completely understand if you believe any of these myths. They are so powerful in society and they could easily be considered cultural norms in their own right, they're that strong in people's minds. And I have believed some of these in the past but that's why I want, need to tackle these head on.

Suicide Myth 1

If you ask someone about suicidal thoughts, it may trigger them to act out.

I'll fully admit that a bunch of these myths we will focus on different sections of the book, and this one does pop up later.

However, for now just know that research shows that by asking someone about suicidal thoughts it will NOT put any ideas into their head that were not already in there. As well as suicidal people want to be asked about and they want to know they matter.

Asking out saves lives 99.9% of the time, so if you're concerned about someone, ask.

Suicide Myth 2

People who talk about suicide never do it.

Now this myth I do understand because in different areas of our social world, it is often the people that bang on about things are the ones that cannot do it. For example, the loudest people that praise how great they are, tend not to be as great as people who don't praise their own achievements.

Things like that.

However, when it's suicide, this is an extremely wrong myth and this easily causes deaths. Since when it comes to suicide, it is the people that do talk about it are the people most likely to do it. That's a major theme through this book.

Therefore, if someone does tell you they're going to self-harm or commit suicide, take it seriously and get them professional help.

Suicide Myth 3

Suicide is an impulsive act.

This is another myth that is completely wrong, and whilst there are sections of this book and research that sort of supports the idea of suicide is related to impulsivity. The vast, vast majority of suicides are planned down to the last detail and suicidal people think about committing suicide for days, weeks or even months before an attempt.

So no, suicide is flat out not an impulsive act and that thinking can harm people because it means others aren't looking out for the warning signs.

Suicide Myth 4

The elderly don't commit suicide.

I suppose in some weird way I can sort of see the twisted logic behind this myth because I think other people believe that because elderly people are, well, elderly they might just wait a few more years anyway to die of natural causes.

However, research shows that the elderly are most likely to complete suicide attempts successfully. And there are other factors that other groups don't always have.

Like losing friends and being alone because they've died, terminal illness, the pain and immobility associated with older age and more.

We all need to remember that suicide is not specific to one group. Suicide can happen to anyone, even if they're in a group with not a lot of extra risk factors.

<u>Suicide Myth 5</u>

Minorities are most likely to commit suicide.

Whilst this seems like a perfectly logical argument at first and it is true these minority groups have risk factors that make them more likely to commit suicide compared to others. It is actually white men that are the most likely to commit suicide due to a range of factors, most of which probably being down to men's inability to get professional help, because of personal and cultural factors as discussed in other chapters.

<u>Suicide Myths 6</u>

Young people aren't at risk of committing suicide. They only use it as a threat to get attention.

If there was one myth that was absolutely outrageous and made me bite my tongue because I wanted to swear so much, it would be this myth.

It is flat out outrageous, ridiculous and utterly pathetic that people dare to think suicide is an attention-seeking mechanism. It is these people that make talking about suicide and the stigma of suicide reinforced, stronger and make sure that people suffer in silence.

As you can tell I hate this myth because as future chapters will show you, it is young people that are *most* at risk of suicide. And by saying that young people are just being attention seekers is outrageous and I truly hope that these awful people realise the damage they are doing in the world by their ignorance.

If I have just insulted you, then I am sorry, and I actually do want to praise you because you are actively finding out more information and that's great. You want to learn and you are probably wanting to find out the truth, it is just a shame that more people aren't like you in this want.

Suicide Myth 7

There's nothing you can do if someone wants to commit suicide.

Personally I have absolutely no idea how this myth came about. I sort of think it may have come about as a way for loved ones, friends and others that learnt about someone's suicidal intent to wash their hands of them and simply not worry about them. And I suppose it could be a coping mechanism for dealing with this new revelation or loss of a loved one, but it is wrong.

Just because someone thinks they want to commit suicide does not mean they are a so-called *lost cause* (hate that idea). We'll talk about it later but there are tons of things you can do to help them, from telling them they are loved and supported, finding them professional help and telling them they are not worthless.

This is covered in a lot more depth in a future chapter, but I just needed to stress that things now.

Suicide Myth 8

Suicide victims always leave a note.

Maybe Hollywood, TV and books are to blame here for that myth but it is only roughly 25% of suicide victims that leave a note. And this unfortunately makes perfect sense because if you believe no one cares about you, you are isolated and lonely, then writing a note will seem truly pointless because you believe no one cares about you so why on earth would they care about reading some note.

Therefore, writing a note seems truly pointless when they already think no one cares about them and others would be better off with them dead.

So they don't do it.

I know it's "nice" to imagine they would leave a note to help give the family closure but that ideal just doesn't match up with the psychological state of suicidal people.

Suicide Myth 9

Anyone who attempts or commits suicide is depressed.

This is another myth I won't go into in too much depth because disproving this myth is basically a theme and one of the purposes of the book, so for now just know there is a wide range of factors that can increase a person's chance to commit suicide.

It is certainly not all down to depression.

Suicide Myth 10

If someone really wants to die we should let them.

I know the vast majority of people here would want to come at this myth from the viewpoint of *all lives are precious and must be saved,* and whilst that is one way to look at the myth.

Another way or reason why this is a myth is because a good amount of suicide survivors realise when they actually do the attempt that they have made a mistake. One great example of this is the author Kevin Hines who jumped off the Golden Gate Bridge, and realised he had made a mistake the second his feet left the concrete.

Final Suicide Myth

Suicide is selfish

I have definitely saved the best myth for last because I am fighting an extremely strong urge here to start swearing because I am so fed up with ignorant people daring to blame the suicide victims for their actions. I am fed up with the stupid beliefs of people who have never ever been suicidal thinking that their actions are rational and these suicide victims are being selfish.

For example, I know tons of people that I love and care about who believe suicidal people are selfish when they want to jump off bridges and the police close the roads.

But this is just outrageous and it shows such ignorance and uncaring towards people that are NOT thinking straight, rationally or see another way out.

No one wants to kill themselves for crying out loud, people only want to kill themselves when they see no other choice because of the wide range of factors.

If the suicidal person wanting to end their live disrupts your day then maybe that is a good thing, because it can only take one single person reaching out to possibly save a life, and not leave a family shattered.

Instead of people blaming the suicide victims for apparently being selfish (what utter rubbish), we need to address why are they feeling like they have no other choice. If it's a factor about society, like a LGBT person being scared about their future, then it is on all of us to take a hard look at ourselves, our neighbourhood and the world we live in to realise what can we do to make sure this doesn't happen again.

And if a person doesn't think suicides can happen again for the same reasons, then I'm sorry but that person needs this book desperately.

HOW SOCIAL FACTORS IMPACT MALE SUICIDE?

After looking at the extremely important topic of suicide myths which as you could tell from that chapter is a passionate area of mine, we need to return to talking about male suicide but in a slightly different way than before.

In this chapter, you'll start to get a sense of the wide range of causes of suicide and most importantly, how social factors impact suicide and what we can hopefully do to prevent it.

A chapter that is definitely worth a read.

***

How Social Factors Impact Male Suicide?

After looking at male suicide as a whole in episode 122, Where we learnt how suicide rates, the general psychology behind suicide and why it's increasing. We now need to investigate a new approach to treating and preventing male suicide. And this will be very eye-opening for all of us!

How Socials Factors Impact Male Suicide?

Like all mental health conditions, male suicide is caused by a number of different interacting factors, but social factors will be the focus of this episode. Simply because these are the factors that can be changed to create more user friendly services for men, building upon the last episode.

Furthermore, the following groups are most likely to be affected by male suicide:

- Unemployed Men
- Divorced Men
- Military Veterans
- Aboriginal Men
- Men with mental health conditions

In addition, the reason why we're looking at these groups of men is simple. For a lesser or greater extent, all these groups share the themes of social isolation, suspicion from wider society, financial strains amongst others. Not only does all this put an additional strain on their mental health, but all these factors can sadly result in wider society giving them a lack of empathy for one reason or another.

All meaning these groups of men are less likely to get the empathy and support they need.

Social Alienation:

This is a particularly awful social factor for everyone, but even more so for these groups of men. Due to when people experience a perceived or real rejection from society then this can lead to a strong sense of social alienation. Leading to the person feeling like they don't have a purpose or meaning in their life anymore.

Both of those are primary reasons for staying alive.

If we use a practical example, in most western countries (the US, UK, France, etc) men tend to get meaning from their lives from two sources. (And yes I know I'm being generic here but it shows the point perfectly) They tend to get meaning and purpose from being in the workforce and being the centre (or head) of a family.

Therefore, when a man loses his family in a divorce or losses his job and becomes unemployed, this can put massive strains on their mental health. As the men could believe they don't have meaning or purpose in their life anymore.

Stereotypes and Male Suicide

Additionally, stereotypes that stigmatise individuals. Like aboriginal men, men with mental health conditions and veterans. These can have even more damaging consequences because these stereotypes lead to people not having as many opportunities for work or dating in the first place, so this leads them to not socially integrate and becoming marginalised.

Leading to social alienation again.

And this is why I hate with a passion stereotypes because most of them are so completely wrong, so they only do more damage for no flaunt of the sufferer. For example, the stupid myth about everyone with a mental health condition is dangerous or depressed people are just lazy.

No!

But hopefully over time these myths, lies and stereotypes will get less and less powerful.

What Does This Mean For Prevention Programmes?

Now we know the information, how do we apply it to the real world and hopefully try to save lives?

If we're going to talk about a new or renewed approach to help prevent male suicide. Then the programme would have to do at least three things.

Firstly, just like the principles of Formulation, we would have to tailor-make the therapy or support to the male in particular. Therefore, the man would get tailored support to their needs to make sure the transition they're undergoing is as easy as possible. Like in a divorce or them becoming unemployed.

Secondly, like I talk about in Abnormal Psychology Third Edition, the psychotherapy or support would have to be adapted to become cultural appropriate since that works best (check out the book for studies). For example, you would have to adapt the therapy given to Aboriginal men in a different way to military veterans to make sure the therapy is as effective as possible.

Finally, the overall mental health service (which is somewhat broken as it due to budget cuts, the focus on the biomedical model and other factors) definitely has a role to play. Since research shows that men prefer grassroots services and local programmes for their mental health, so support through be developed through local services.

Some of these grassroots places include spiritual or religious organisations, local peer-to-peer support groups and other non-profits. As well as these organisations are actually well placed to help with mental health, the feelings of social alienation and loss of meaning and purpose in life.

Wrap Up

After covering the basics of male suicide, I know that there is a lot that needs to change in the world before the silent crisis of male suicide can start to slow down, and hopefully stop one day. But I really hope by talking about the psychology of suicide on the podcast, I can start to educate people about it. (And educate myself too)

In the following suicide-based podcast episodes, we'll start to look at the really interesting aspects of suicide and cover aspects I had no idea were related to suicide. So fascinating episodes ahead!

But please, if you, your friends or anyone you know ever thinks about suicide, please seek professional help.

SUICIDE PSYCHOLOGY

HOW DOES DEPRESSION IMPACT SUICIDE?

Whilst a lot of this book will focus on mental health and other wide ranging factors that can increase the chance of people committing suicide, before we go any further we need to at least be introduced to the topic of mental health.

Therefore, this is another podcast episode from early in 2022 that focuses on depression and how that impacts suicide by focusing on 3 questions surrounding the topic.

How Does Depression Impact Suicide? 3 Questions Answered

After looking at suicide already in a lot of depth, we need to consider how depression affects suicide. Since as always there are a lot of myths and misconceptions about how depression impacts suicide, so in this psychology podcast episode, that is exactly what we seek to look at. How does Depression impact suicide?

<u>How Does Depression Impact Suicide?</u>
<u>How Does Depression Lead To Suicidal Thinking?</u>

Lots of different people experience suicidal thinking in their life and this usually happens after a difficult life event. Like the loss of a loved one, job or something else that is important to them, as we've spoken about on previous episodes.

In addition, depression links to this type of thinking because it impairs our cognitive flexibility as it changes our patterns of feeling and thinking so we cannot see a way out of our current situation. As well as we cannot imagine or even entertain the idea of a better future.

Also the Cognitive Triad in depression leads a person to focus on all their setbacks, all their so-called mistakes and what makes them a failure. Including relationship failures and adverse childhood experiences. Therefore, this only adds to their feelings of worthlessness and depression that only magnifies the pain they're suffering.

All leading to a depressed person being more likely to seek out suicide as the only viable escape route from all this suffering and psychological pain.

Personally, this is rather tragic to write about but it is important. It is important for all of us to understand the importance of treatment and the work we do as psychology professionals and in the future psychology students. It is the work we do that can save lives, or at the very least help people decrease and cope with their psychological distress.

This is why psychology is critical.

How Common Is Suicide In Depression?

According to the U.S Department of Health and Human Services, it turns out 2% of people who are treated for depression in an outpatient service take their own life. As well as out of all those people who were ever hospitalised for depression, the death rate by suicide is 4%.

Before I go on to dive into the numbers a bit more, I just wanted to mention that this does sort of fly in the face of a massive misconception about suicide. Since I have heard plenty of times through the grapevine so to speak that people believe that all depressed people commit suicide.

Thankfully that is far, far, far from the case. But still 4% is too high for my liking. It should be 0% in an ideal world and thankfully that is where psychologists come in.

Additionally, around 60% of suicide victims have a mood condition that is potentially treatable and younger people who kill themselves often have a substance abuse difficulty as well. Of course, in addition, to the other life factors that can impact suicide.

And this is the main reason why I talk about all these things in my books, in-person and on the podcast. Because even if I can educate or prompt one person to convince others to get professional help if they have a mental health condition, then that means I could have potentially saved a life.

This is why psychologists and therapists are critical because without us so many people would still be suffering.

As well as this is why I hate with a passion all the rubbish that psychology gets. With people thinking we know nothing, psychology is profiling and therapists are dangerous (as in villains in TV and books). Because this bad representation isn't helpful to us, our clients and the people who need professional aid but don't trust us.

Anyway jumping off my soapbox now!

Do Anti-Suicide Pacts Work?

Wow!

This is actually rather cool and rather clever.

So these pacts have been around for ages between at-risk patients and therapists as a way to stop the patient from committing suicide. These pacts or contracts can be written or verbal but that isn't important. What is important is that it gets the at-risk patient to not self-harm or commit suicide.

As well as the pacts make the patient call the therapist, an emergency number or 999 if they even think about suicide for a moment.

Furthermore, effective suicide contracts which are written, dated and signed with a copy given to each person and kept in an accessible location. Not only ensure the patient doesn't kill themselves but it ensures they call emergency numbers when they're in danger.

Again what is so brilliant about these pacts is they are not legally binding so that increases comfort for the patient. As the therapist cannot and does not need to file it in court and get the patient arrested. Because of course, suicide is a crime.

Also this is already very commonplace in certain industries where the suicidal rates are extremely high. Like in paramedics and other first responders, with them becoming more and more common amongst friends and family members of anyone who has been suicidal.

And this is what I love about this podcast, because I think this pact is utterly amazing. It is such an effective and easy to do method that I'm extremely pleased that people have this option.

Conclusion:

After today's episode, I'm actually... rather hopeful about the future because if this episode has taught me anything. It is how important psychology students (for the future) and psychology professionals are, because we are a massive line of defence for depressed people.

Also I guess that was the real point for today's episode, it was to teach all of us how valuable we are for depressed people, and why our work matters so much to so many.

And I have to admit I love those anti-suicide pacts. I think they're a great idea. Of course, nothing on the podcast is ever official advice, but they're still pretty great.

SUICIDE AND PRISONS

If you've ever listened to my podcast or any
other of my books then you know that I love forensic
psychology in its own right and as a subfield of
clinical psychology, so I suppose that it would be
impossible for me not to look into how forensic
psychology and suicide overlapped.

And in terms of this book, I wanted to change
our perspective a little, just so we're looking at
something completely different before we dive into
other topics.

You seriously cannot get further away from the
things we have previously looked at (to some extent)
than looking at suicidality in criminals.

Enjoy.

***

Stepping away from clinical psychology and
looking at suicide through that lens, we now need to
look at how the forensic psychology of suicide by
looking at criminals and suicide. I have spoken about

this in my Forensic Psychology book, but in today's podcast episode we're going to look at it from another angle. This is going to be really, really interesting!

Suicide and Prisons

There are two "danger zones" for suicide when it comes to criminals. The first is when they are arrested and taken to jail at the police station or something like this before they go to prison. As well as the second danger zone is when they go to prison itself.

Both of these situations and places are suicidal danger zones (especially in the first 24 hours) because the criminal's future looks so uncertain to them. And as we spoke about in the last podcast episode on suicide, is that uncertainty about the future and inability to see a better one, that leads to suicidal ideation. Then the attempt itself.

As a result, this is why suicide rates in prisons are extremely high compared to the outside world.

But besides from the lack of a certain future, what other factors increase the risk of suicide in prisons?

Crying Wolf:

Now of course the crying wolf title isn't anything official but it is an easy way to imagine what the research shows. For example, we have all seen at least once or twice a TV programme or film where the prisoner screams about their in pain, they need to see a doctor or they're going to kill themselves if something doesn't happen. Then if someone does help them then they are attacked and the prisoners escape.

In reality, this rarely happens but because it is overly used in Television. It sort of becomes part of our collective knowledge so we expect it to happen. This doesn't help the situation, especially considering what I say below.

This does happen in the real world and sadly there are inmates that fake real suicide ideation. Leading to the prison officers to conclude that all prisoners are simply crying wolf and are lying. Meaning no prison officers are going to help them.

Personally I can understand this because even the most compassionate prison officers can become immune to these cries for help. And then if you read into forensic psychology and the workplace culture of prisons, then you learn that it is understandable for the officers not to be too helpful towards the inmates. Unfortunately.

Hardening Officers:

As I mentioned in the above section, over time as a compassionate and hopeful new prison officer gets to experience prisoners and what work is actually like inside a prison. This can lead to them hardening their attitudes towards the inmates making them harsher, stricter and generally less likely to believe them and this affects their judgements too.

Again I do understand this because it isn't easy working in a prison. And you must have to deal with some truly horrible people on the more extreme end of the scale. Then again, you get to work with some good people too that have simply made a bad choice.

But as we know from Cognitive and Social Psychology, we always tend to remember the bad more than the good.

In addition, it is terrible that "just dessert" sentiments flow free in our society. Meaning even if a prison officer believes the criminal will commit suicide they may not bother trying to prevent it, because it is what they deserve.

Prolonged Sentences:

A final reason for suicide in prisons can be linked to inmates who are serving a prolonged prison sentence. For example, a life sentence or a whole life sentence. As this prolonged length of prison time can make inmates think that suicide is a reasonable reaction to such a sentence. And interestingly people on the outside believe it too.

Of course there are more people that serve long prison sentences and do not commit suicide, but depression and suicidality are common like we spoke about before.

What Is Done?

All prisons have different processes in place for suicidal inmates but there are problems with everything. For example, in one place if an inmate was seen to be suicidal, they would have their cell stripped of every single thing that could be used to end themselves with. Even their sheets and mattress, so the inmate was given a strange foam thing to cover themselves with at night.

But inmates can still climb up on their sink and jump. That's all I'm going to say about that.

In addition, if suicidal inmates don't stop in their ideation then they can be moved to hospitals for treatment. And lots of other complicated and unfortunately bureaucratic processes can happen too.

However, what is interesting is Joseph H. Baskin, M.D says that impulsivity suicidal inmates are actually easier to work with because they want to be helped and regarded. So it might be easier to reach out, form a therapeutic relationship and help them.

But still, the combination of hopelessness and impulsivity is deadly.

Conclusion:

Forensic psychology will always be one of my favourite areas of psychology. But this is both a fascinating and tragic topic to look at, because retribution doesn't get us anywhere so these "just dessert" sentiments are deadly. And even though these people have made bad choices, it doesn't mean they need to commit suicide.

So hopefully in the future more can be done to help prevent this, and decrease the alarmingly high suicide rate amongst prisoners.

STIGMA AND SUICIDE

To finish up the introductory content and before we move onto completely new content, I really wanted to share with you a reflection from my Clinical Psychology Reflections Volume 3 book because in that book I reflect a little on suicide, stigma and clinical psychology.

At best, I really hope this gives the book a bit more depth and it helps give you a new perspective.

At worse, I hope you enjoy this reflection.

***

Stigma and Suicide

I've been wanting to do this reflection for a rather long time now but I have just never felt ready to reflect on such a topic, but given how I'll be writing a psychology of suicide book at some point this year, I thought this would be a good way to dive into the topic.

And sometimes you just need to get on and actually do something, like this reflection.

Of course, there are a lot of different angles to look at when it comes to suicide but I really want to focus on the stigma angle.

In addition, I want to mention first of all that when a person decides to try and commit suicide. They don't want to do it, but they feel like they have absolutely no other choice, they've been abandoned by everything they love and they feel like a burden to their loved ones and friends.

And this is actually something that really, really annoys me about people when it comes to talking about suicide. Since if there is a jumper or someone learns about a person who has committed suicide, they tend to be indifferent or blaming the victim.

To some extremely limited extent, I can sort of "understand" where they are coming from. Since if you're driving to work or coming back from work and the authorities close the motorway (or highway for our international audience) because someone is going to jump off the bridge.

Then I can sort of see how that would be annoying and make the drivers angry because apparently the jumper is being selfish about their choice to kill themselves.

Thus, blaming the suicide victim for their behaviour.

Furthermore, the whole conversation in society about how selfish suicide is as a way to die is rather... no, extremely unhelpful because again it is blaming the victim. It is blaming the victim for not doing certain things, not being strong enough and all that other societal rubbish that makes mental health sufferers feel like they cannot reach out or get help.

However, the biggest problem with all of these victim blaming arguments is that they assume that a suicidal person is just as rational, logical and psychologically stable as the non-suicidal people that are blaming them.

But they aren't.

Due to if evolution and our biology has taught us anything, it is how badly humans are wired to survive. Humans are an innate drive to live and survive no matter what, so for a person to overcome our most primal instinct, it's bad.

No one wants to commit suicide, no one wants to end their life but suicidal people feel like they have absolutely no choice that the world is better off without them.

I have no idea how non-suicidal people think that screams logical, rational or psychologically stable. Because it flat out doesn't.

And this just goes to show how little people care or want to help suicidal people because if they did then they would at least have the common sense to realise that they do need psychological help. And they shouldn't be blamed.

You only need to research into the reasons why people want to kill themselves to know how wide ranging it is. From mental health to financial reasons to relationship problems and more. There is no such thing as a typical suicidal person, but they all need psychological help and people to support them.

Additionally, in the UK, because our governments are kept cutting back on mental health services for services and they are failing to get our services back in working order. Our mental health services do not have the time, money or resources to help people until they are suicidal.

Meaning if someone is depressed or suffers from another mental health condition and they come into a mental health service wanting help. Most of the time the NHS has to turn them away until it is a lot worse.

So when that same person tries to commit suicide a few months later, everyone in clinical psychology knows we should have seen that person months ago, but because of the state of the NHS and the lack of political will to do anything about it. This cycle of turning away people and leaving them to get worse will only continue.

Of course, none of these reflections are ever meant to be negative or I always like to put a positive spin on them towards the end. But I'm afraid even I can't be positive on a topic like this, because it is simply ridiculous that us as a society we are blaming people who are suicidal. When in actual fact we should be blaming the system that is failing us as future or current psychologists, and failing them.

And to make matters worse, this mental health crisis will only get worse and worse as time goes on. The mental health crisis was really bad before the pandemic, but the backlog of referrals only spiralled out of control during the COVID-19 pandemic.

Therefore, whilst it is flat out not our fault or the fault of our clients, something needs to be done.

Personally, this is why I'm looking forward to writing my book on the psychology of suicide just so I can see possible routes for the future, and how to prevent suicide. As well as I also hope that there will be structural changes within the NHS to help these problems and there will be a political change just so our politicians do start investing and caring about mental health and suicide more.

There is a lot to do, and I really hope something changes soon.

HOW TO TALK ABOUT SUICIDAL THOUGHTS?

Now that we have the basic information done, I just really, really want to put this chapter next because it is so critical. This is very much one of the most important chapters in this entire book, because before now and later in the book, I will mention how important it is for reaching out to loved ones and suicidal people.

But how on earth do you do that?

And I need to stress upfront that this chapter is for BOTH people considering suicide and for people who are concerned about a loved one. It is written with both groups of people in mind, and of course nothing in this book is never any sort of official advice.

I'm writing it that way because I don't want anyone to perceive me as making it sound easier than it is, because it really isn't. And I don't want people without suicidal experience to underestimate how difficult these conversations are.

Therefore, let me be very extremely clear here, talking about suicidal thoughts is extremely difficult for everyone involved and this widespread discomfort stems from our cultural norms. Since we still sadly live in a society where you simply do not talk about suicide because it is a taboo subject.

A subject that because it is taboo costs lives. Hence why I'm writing this book in the first place.

In addition, talking about suicidal thoughts as the person who has them or is concerned about a loved one, is a deeply emotionally painful experience to consider suicide.

It's painful for the person to suicide committing suicide because they feel that hopeless.

It's painful for the person concerned about a loved one, because no one likes to imagine their loved one feeling like this.

As a result, you might not know how to bridge the conversation and make these feelings come to light. This is a perfectly normal reaction and it really does not make you a bad person for feeling like this.

In fact, it's natural as the vast majority of people are hesitant to talk about this topic as well as people with suicidal thoughts may quit the idea of having this conversation out of fear of burdening loved ones.

Which is not correct, you are not a burden as you'll see later on in the chapter.

Additionally, the silence in our society only maintains the stigma and pushes those people with these suicidal thoughts into further isolation.

However, being willing to bridge the subject could help someone at risk towards very much needed help and start their journey towards emotional recovery. That's why this chapter is so important because it is so powerful.

And as always and as we're focusing on the powerful conversations, it is always better to reach out and maybe save a life than stay silent and risk a death.

Furthermore, anyone who is suspecting that a close other is thinking about suicide should talk to them but this is of course easier said than done. This is what we need to focus on now.

Since starting off this conversation can definitely seem impossible, because you will feel anxious and apprehensive at the idea. Suicidal people will feel like this because they're seeing the situation through their feelings of sadness, feeling worthless and being a burden with their loved ones being better off without them.

Concerned people will feel like this because they're scared of finding their fears are true, but they love the suicidal person and want to help them.

How To Talk About Suicidal Thoughts For People Concerned About A Loved One?

As well as it's important to note that actually talking about it in an open way and honest way is one of most powerful weapons to fight against it, and it's key to understanding that someone is struggling more than loved one can ever imagine.

Also there's decades of research that shows social support and suicide makes one thing clear, when in doubt, reach out.

Another helpful tip about approaching this topic could be to write some conversation tips down beforehand and this is a way to help manage anxiety and make you feel more in control. The exact same goes for formulating a plan and feeling empowered to start the conversation.

Moreover, it has to be mentioned that you certainly don't need to be a trained psychologist or mental health professional to start the conversation, just make sure after the conversation you help them connect with mental health services. But it might be a great idea to learn about risk factors and more about suicide, and as you're reading this book I hope you're okay on that front.

At the end of the day, you do not need to say the perfect thing and you won't be able to solve everything in one conversation, yet reaching out will help your loved one feel understood and it's likely the first step to recovery. And it could save their life further down the road.

Additionally, as we know from the second chapter, asking about suicide doesn't put the idea in their head, it's a myth, and a vast body of literature shows open conversations are unlikely to increase suicidal ideation.

It actually has the immense power to decrease it,

especially when done with empathy and coupled with additional mental health support.

If after starting the conversation and if the loved one admits thoughts of hurting themselves, experts stress don't act shocked or horrified as this only creates distance and could make the loved one feel judged.

That isn't what you want.

Also it might be tempting to jump straight to problem-solving, but at this point it's important to see and listen without judgement and be empathic. As well as make an effort to validate their feelings. For example, by even saying something like, "I'm so sorry you're feeling so hopeless—it must be horrible" can be very powerful.

What you absolutely mustn't do is say they have no reason for feeling this way. That is flat out stupid, it will only reinforce the idea that no one cares about them, they're worthless and the world is better off without them.

Do not do that.

Afterwards this, it is absolutely critical to connect them with mental health support services.

Sharing Suicidal Thoughts With Others

This is extremely hard, I know, and it takes such immense amounts of courage to do this but it is critical, and in many cases such worries that the suicidal person has are far from true with many people they're close with are willing and able to help if only given the chance.

It is hard to reach out that is absolutely no denying that and if anyone says it is easy, then they are lying. Plain and simple. But no one is alone in this world and it is does not matter how dark the world seems with horrible people, wars and situations that seem impossible to escape from. There will always be people who are looking to help, support and care about you.

You are never alone.

This sharing does require a massive act of courage, and it is a valuable, if not critical, first step towards getting help and restoring your well-being. It is helpful to try to be as direct as possible, tell them how you're struggling with feelings of hopelessness, depression, worthlessness and any other things you're feeling.

The person you're telling might become emotional or respond with shock, and this will be a shock to you too because this might not be the reaction you wanted. This is why preparing ahead of time for any possible reaction can help you maintain composure and continue this conversation.

Continuing is just critical.

Then tell them what you need. Like help finding a therapist? Wanting them to be there for you? Listening to your challenges and offer emotional support.

At the end of the day, your loved ones care about you, and they may need to let others know about this, but please don't be frustrated with them because they are only doing what they believe is best for you.

It's valuable to take some time to prepare for this sort of conversation because this will help you to soothe your anxiety or any guilt in you, and this could allow you to become more proactive.

Yet if it is easy for you to get lethal means or the suicidal thoughts become persistent, do not prepare, just get help. Have the conversation.

However, sometimes it is too uncomfortable or you're unable to talk to loved ones because you actually know they won't respond well, or they believe you have no reason to feel like this.

Then DO NOT lose hope either.

Instead there are a lot of great suicide prevention hotlines that you can call for free, confidential help and they can provide emotional support and concrete assistance in getting more help for you.

Of course, no one can ever force anyone to share their thoughts with others, but many people who reach out to loved ones end up having a very worthwhile experience. Since struggling with suicidal thoughts is extremely isolating, and social connection can be a powerful source of comfort and relief.

And while it is true that sharing thoughts will lead others to worry, just like how you would be worried if they said the same to you. But we all forget sometimes that worry isn't about being a burden, it is a sign of love and that they care about you and want you to do well.

None of us worry about things we don't care

about, so if your loved ones worry about you then that's a good sign. Because they love you and you aren't a burden.

It is best to share your thoughts, struggles and feelings regardless of your loved one's penchant for worry, and remember you're in control of what you share and how you share it.

Interestingly, if you're worried about how they'll respond, it can be helpful to have the conversation over phone or email, rather than face to face.

Do whatever allows you to share your thoughts and get what you need without focusing excessively on how others are responding emotionally.

And if you don't feel safe about sharing and reaching out, it is a great shame that some people don't respond well, so please reach out to a friend instead and if that's not possible, then reach out to a trusted community member. They may be able to provide emotional support and connect you with resources.

And remember sharing is critical in the journey to recovery and suicide hotlines are critical.

I'll repeat it. Suicide hotlines are critical.

WHAT ARE THE SIGNS SOMEONE IS THINKING ABOUT SUICIDE?

In a way I fully admit it might have made more sense to put this chapter before the last one, but personally I just really, really wanted to put the talking about suicide chapter as soon into the book as possible. And in a way, now that we know how to talk and the importance of the signs, this chapter seems a bit more relevant now.

Especially as the last chapter basically proved that it is possible to talk to suicidal people.

Therefore, spotting the signs that someone is thinking about committing suicide is uniquely challenging, and this only highlights the fact that when someone does lose a loved one to suicide, it doesn't mean they were bad parents, family members or they or the therapist was derelict in their duty.

It's hard to spot or recognise the signs.

It is also slightly helpful in this case that some people thankfully vocalise their intentions and externally show what they intend to do before they actually do it. Other people sadly conceal and hide their intentions, so it is a lot harder to recognise the signs.

In addition, it is flat out impossible to know what's going on in a person's head, none of us are mind readers. Yet it is always a good idea to ask if you see any warning signs or you suspect that the loved one might be thinking about suicide. Better safe than sorry.

And it is always better safe than sorry. Better to ask and get them to look at you funny and confused about why you would ask them. Then ask not, and lose them forever.

In terms of warning signs, there are a lot of common ones that you can watch out for. Of course, this will never be a complete list but some of these might be very useful to you in the future or right now.

If a person makes a will, tries to get "their affairs in order" and gives away personal possessions then this on its own might not be a warning sign, but when coupled with other signs, it is.

Secondly, if your loved one talks about feeling worthless, trapped, hopeless and like they have no reasons to keep living. And this is why it was important to have the last chapter first, because if you come across this particular warning sign then you know how to breach the topic.

Thirdly, if the loved one sleeps too little or too much that could be a sign of depression and other mental health conditions, and if they eat too much or too little. As well as if they have attempted suicide or shown suicidal behaviour in the past, then that is a clear warning sign they could do it in the future.

In addition, if they search for ways to harm themselves, then that is cause for concern. For example, if they search how to buy a gun or access dangerous medication, as well as if the loved one shows signs of despair or they have significant mood swings.

Here are some other warning signs:

- Have experienced a severe life stressor recently. For example, the death of a spouse or other loved one, the loss of a job or a traumatic event.
- Drinks alcohol or uses drugs excessively.
- Avoids other people, including loved ones; spends more time than usual alone.
- Acts agitated, anxious, or aggressive.
- They behave recklessly.

Of course, it needs to be mentioned that absolutely none of these are perfect indicators, but these are common signs within suicidal people, and they are critical to watch out for.

Are You At Risk Of Suicide?

One of the points of the book is try and be as honest with everyone as possible, and cater for different groups of people. And this is where the honesty comes in, because it turns out that most people at some point in their life will experience passing suicidal thoughts. Even if it is as simple as you being really furious with someone and you thinking *I wish I had never been born.*

If this thought happens then just bear in mind the predictors and try to manage your thoughts, like always focus on the positive.

However, if these suicidal thoughts stop becoming so passing and they become persistent. Then definitely take them seriously, as well as anytime they become noticeable or concerning, definitely seek help.

As a result of even if the person doesn't have a plan for suicide when these thoughts occur, a sudden spike in suicidal thinking likely suggests a larger mental health difficulty or a life challenge that can be productively addressed if you seek help.

And as always there is absolutely no shame in seeking help. It doesn't make you weak, silly or anything else that societal rubbish teaches us about mental health not being real health. I hate it when people preach those lies.

Additionally, even if the person's suicidal ideation hasn't shifted or moved from passive (thinking about committing suicide) to active (planning and making preparations for it), it's still a good idea to talk to a loved one or a therapist about these thoughts. Due to this is the first step to overcoming them, strengthening your mental well-being and starting a journey of recovery.

Also, it's worth noting that many people in psychotherapy with different mental health conditions are scared about telling their therapists that they have these suicidal thoughts.

Some of these fears are rather logical in a way because they are scared about their friends and family being told, and they're concerned about immediately being committed to an in-patient programme and they won't be able to go home that day.

However, please rest assured that mental health professionals are trained to handle these discussions without judgement or rash action. Meaning the fears are unfounded and this is a good thing that the client wants to tell the therapists.

Also a good therapist responds to this conversation with compassion and calm to make the whole experience better for the client. And as I always say, in clinical psychology, our job is to work with our clients to decrease their psychological distress and improve their lives.

Acting with compassion and calm is one of the ways we can do that.

Finally, in reality, in most cases the client is asked a few follow-up questions to help the therapist understand what's going on. For example, they probably be asked whether their suicide is in the passive or active stage, do they have a specific plan and do they have a readily accessible means of suicide.

After if the therapist concludes that the client isn't at an immediate risk, then they will likely work with them to develop a safety plan in case the thoughts escalate to an attempt. Meantime, in the therapy sessions the psychotherapist and client will explore the source of the suicidal thoughts and help to develop alternative coping mechanisms for the feelings of despair as well as hopelessness.

But the entire point of the chapter is two-fold. Firstly, even though there are not perfect indicators of suicidal intent, there are plenty to be aware of just in case.

And secondly, if you ever feel like you have passing thoughts of suicide, monitor them and make sure you get help if they become persistent.

HOW LGBT HATE CRIMES LINK WITH SUICIDE?

After the past few rather heavy chapters, I wanted to do a sort of lighter chapter in a way. Because whilst all suicide chapters are not positive in the slightest, this chapter has a more hopeful tone that definitely helped me to feel better after the past few chapters.

Personally I strongly believe this would be an absolutely awful book on suicide if we covered a lot of other things and not the high rate of LGBT deaths. This is something that scares me, I hate that people do not accept people from the LGBT community and there are places in the world were LGBT people feel so scared that they see suicide as their only option.

This is common and just flat out outrageous and I hate the findings of this chapter more than I could ever put into words.

On the off chance that an LGBT person is reading this chapter, all I can say is I know how scary the world seems at times and how much hate we can get, but you are loved and you are never alone.

How Hate Crimes Link With Suicide?

Moving onto the very important content, hate crimes, to oversimplify, are crimes done against a particular community or group of people and are designed to terrorise them, and are motivated by the offender's hate for that group.

In addition, the reasoning behind hate crime laws is twofold. Since the first reason for these laws is because the crimes are motivated by prejudice and hate, as well as they are especially harmful because they are designed to terrorise an entire community, not just direct victims.

Which is definitely a major way in how they differ from "normal" crimes. Typically crimes are designed to harm direct victims. Like the shoplifting only really hurts the shop owners, not the entire community of shop owners. But hate crimes don't work like that.

Secondly, the victims of these hate crimes are typically people from protected classes, with these being populations that have suffered and continue to suffer victimisation and discrimination.

Therefore, these crimes are committed against specific groups of people because of their minority status. Resulting in additional psychological harm to them, and this is both above and beyond the criminal harm per se.

Furthermore, whilst the political issue hate

legislation is a question of public values and policy, and a whole bunch of other utterly ridiculous things that can stop these protective laws from coming into force.

What we're interested in is the scientific question about work of connecting hate crimes to harm and this can be pursued in a variety of innovative research methods. Since it's all well and good wanting to bring in hate crime laws, but what's the point if hate crime doesn't harm people?

Hence the need to research them and find out if hate crimes does actually harm people from minority groups.

As a result, this work brings together scientists from a wide range of areas. Such as teams from public health, sociology, criminology, psychology and others.

Just like professor Dustin Duncan at Harvard and now New York University, who lead a team of researchers interrogating the question of whether anti-LGBT hate crimes does harm the mental health of LGBT community. With their particular focus being on adolescents because this is the group with the highest suicide rate. Especially with the acceptance of being LGBT is a difficult time.

To do this the researchers examined at a number of levels, but Dr Ducan looked at the community-level data. More specifically the researchers mapped the reports of anti-LGBT hate crimes through the Boston area, and looked at the correlation between those hate crimes and suicide attempts by adolescents in the Boston area.

The results found that in "hot spot" areas of anti-LGBT bias and hate, there was an increased level of suicidality among LGBT youth.

This was confirmed by the analysis showing that poor mental health outcomes were specific to LGBT adolescents in these areas, not just young people overall. Due to that's a very important finding, because with research we can say that hate crime does increase suicide levels within the targeted community, and not the general population. Hence the need for hate crime laws.

As well as if we want to get very technical about these results, the public health terms for this is we would say the correlation is specific, not spurious.

Finally, because I promised a slightly more positive chapter at the start, I want to stress here to both LGBT people and non-LGBT people some things.

If you're not LGBT and these results don't affect you then I'm really pleased, and I would definitely encourage you to always be aware of this issue, challenge hate crimes and support minority groups. Because as we know from other chapters, the lack of support and hopelessness leads to suicide, and everyone can help prevent that if we confront it head on.

If you are LGBT then please know that things can get better. You can have an amazing life filled with love, respect and whatever you want. You are not deranged, possessed or whatever else the bible-bashers want to call you. You are an amazing person that is capable of so much and you are never ever alone.

There's a reason why LGBT is called a community. Sure it is hard to find sometimes, but there is a community that will love, support and respect you for sure.

There is always another way.

WHAT IS THE SUICIDE RISK OF CHILDREN, TEENAGERS AND YOUNG PEOPLE?

Whilst this might be the tenth chapter for you to enjoy, this is actually the last chapter for me because I felt the massive need to write this last. Personally I don't know why but after writing the rest of the book, I now know how critical this chapter is to the rest of the book.

Therefore, whilst I fully agree with you that this is a heart-wrecking topic. It is just so critical to fully understanding suicide, why people do it and helping to fight some of the absolutely outrageous myths that suicide makes up.

Let's begin.

As you can imagine the very idea of a child dying by suicide is simply unimaginable to many parents. It stirs up such a range of emotions and it can still people with such crippling grief.

However, a significant number of children do

seriously think or attempt suicide, and this is one of the leading causes of death in children and teenagers. As well as whilst the evidence thankfully suggests that suicide is rare, it is becoming more common place.

As a result of this evidence, parents need to be aware of the key warning signs (there is a section dedicated to this later in the book), knowing what behavioural changes to look for, how to ask and how to find support for these children and teenagers. Which is something we have all looked at in this book together.

And it's important to know that this knowledge isn't meant to be scary, it's meant to be empowering for families, because with this knowledge families can provide emotional support to their child, know how to respond to their needs and put them on the road to recovery.

But I know I have mentioned throughout the book, and I will keep saying this, but if a child does commit suicide, it flat out doesn't mean the parents were bad.

There are a lot of non-parental risk factors.

More Introduction:

In my research this section was a little further down but I needed to bring it up here to give it the most impact.

Therefore, Janiri et al. (2020) found that 8% 9-to-10 year olds reported experiencing past or current suicidal thoughts with slightly more than 1% of this age group attempting suicide. As well as other research suggests that roughly 1 in 8 children between 6 and 12 experience suicidal thoughts.

And whilst it is completely impossible for us to think about this, children as young as five have been known to experience suicidal thoughts and small number of these young children die each year by suicide.

Furthermore, another study Bridge et al. (2015) found that less than 2 in every million children between 5 and 11 die by suicide. Yet Adolescents older than 12 die by suicide a rate of approximately 52 per million.

Overall, whilst this is extremely distressing to think about, it is just critical to remember that the risk is real, and very small. And none of this chapter is meant to scare parents or people who want to become parents in the future.

Parents can mitigate any potential danger by taking seriously any talk from their child about death, feeling like a burden, self-harm or feeling hopeless. Also it's important to talk to children about their feelings and fears, as well as making it clear that the parents are available whenever the child needs help, and if necessary, the parents are proactively seeking mental health care if their child needs it.

What Children Are At Risk?

Of course it is worth reminding ourselves that despite the evidence that child suicide is coming more common, in the grand scheme of things most children don't commit suicide, so the overall risk for an individual is low.

For children, their suicide risk factors are a little different to adults because of their age but there is some overlap too. For example, certain factors like age, family dynamics, peer relationships, mental health and gender may increase the risk of suicide.

That's why it's critical for teachers, parents and other adult authority figures to keep this in the back of their mind just in case they need this information. Especially if the warning signs show up.

For all of us, it is not always easy to answer as to why a child or teenager has suicidal thoughts. There are some risk factors like being bullied, neglected, experiencing sexual or physical abuse or other trauma that help to explain it.

Some of the reasons include feeling lonely or socially isolated as well as struggling with a mental health condition. Like depression, bipolar, ADHD or anxiety.

In terms of looking beyond mental health conditions, significant feelings of stress, anger, sadness, or self-doubt and feeling as if they have no one to turn to all increased the risk of suicide.

Additionally, if a child or teenager has lost a loved one, this is a factor that could heighten the risk, and the same goes for a child with recently divorced parents or if their families are facing serious financial trouble.

Furthermore, if there is a lot of family conflict then research shows this is a greater risk factor for young children. But once the child reaches their teen years, conflict with their peers begin to have a more significant effect on mental health than it used to.

And as we looked at in the last chapter, if the teenage or tweens identify themselves as a sexual or gender minority or they're questioning their sexual orientation then this does heightened risk for suicidal ideation. Not because of the identification itself but because of all the societal nonsense surrounding it, like homosexuality is abnormal and they're abominations, and this is all before we consider these risk factors may be exacerbated by being bullied or feeling unsupported by their social support network.

Sadly if we turn our attention to young children for a moment, it is more common for this younger age group to take their lives impulsively, this of course happens in other age groups, but it is more common for young children. This is because they may not know how to cope with difficult feelings and their brains aren't yet developed enough to properly manage their impulses.

In the grand scheme of things, suicide of young children is rare, and limiting access to lethal means can significantly reduce the risk of a child harming themselves suddenly.

And personally I was not going to include this in the book but all the research articles and blog posts and more that I researched for this book kept coming back to locking up guns, handguns and semi-automatic weapons.

Personally, I don't care what you believe or what your stance on gun control is, but as a person who lives in the United Kingdom, everyone (or a very good chunk of people) having a gun is just a strange concept that I flat out don't understand.

But in the interest of trying to unofficially keep as many people safe as possible, LOCK UP YOUR GUNS. It is not hard to lock them up and just keep them away from children to keep them safe and if it's harder to get to the guns then it's harder for them to commit suicide.

I've said it. I've probably annoyed a bunch of people, but I'm writing this book to try to save lives. So I really don't care if I've offended your gun beliefs.

LOCK THEM UP AND SAVE LIVES!

Teenage Suicides:

All the research for the next three paragraphs is from a CDC report published in 2020, if you want to see it all please check out the reference section later in the book.

Anyway, it is a lot more common for teenagers to commit suicide than younger children, because 19% of teenagers self-reported they were seriously considering suicide in 2019, and 9% of teenagers reported attempting suicide in the same period.

Now unlike adults, research suggests that teenage girls are more likely to commit suicide, with them being twice as likely as boys.

Additionally, as mentioned earlier, if a teenager identifies as Lesbian, Gay or Bisexual then this sharply increased the risk with nearly 47% of these teenagers reporting they seriously considered suicide in 2019 and 23% reported they attempted it.

However, this suicide and gender link amongst teenage suicides gets a little stranger for researchers, because research has consistently shown that girls are more likely to attempt suicide than boys, but it is the boys who are more likely to die.

Leading researchers to call this the so-called "suicide gender paradox". This is often attributed to boys' greater propensity to choose more lethal means. Whereas girls tend to use less violent means where their chances of survival are greater.

On the other hand, there is some recent evidence suggesting that the gender gap could be narrowing, at least amongst teenagers, because the suicide rates of teenage girls are higher than in the past. The reason behind this increase appears to be driven by a shift to more lethal means by girls.

Although, it has to be mentioned again like different experts emphasise, regardless of a person's gender, their suicide ideations and thoughts should be taken seriously and responded to rapidly.

You only need to look at the rest of the book to find out how deadly it is when these thoughts are ignored.

Social Media

I definitely feel like some people would be a little disappointed if I didn't mention social media at least once in this book. Then again, there will be readers who, at no fault of their own, believe that social media is absolutely evil when it comes to suicide. And my response to that is a very typical response that most lecturers give students.

Yes. Maybe. No. It depends.

I say this because social media isn't always bad and it does actually have a lot of benefits for youth. For instance, it improves communication, helps them to develop new interests and it broadens social networks. The problem is when they start to substitute online for real-world connections and activities.

As seen as in a 2017 study from the Royal Society of Public Health and Young Health Movement, in their study they examined 506,820 young people that were aged 13 to 18, and found that adolescents who spent more time on screens had a significantly higher likelihood of experiencing depressive symptoms or having at least one suicide-related outcome.

And the overarching point of the study was that balance is absolutely critical. Since the study found teenagers using electronic devices three or more hours a day had a 34% higher chance of at least 1 suicide-related outcome than those using devices two or less hours a day. As well as adolescents who visited social media sites every day were 13% more likely to report high levels of depressive symptoms.

Moreover, according to research, the popularity measures done by social media companies contribute to depression, because these may lead to feelings of inadequacy when young people see their "friends" having a good time.

Although, this isn't true for all users because if a teenager is well-adjusted, the effect may be the opposite, and it boosts their positive feelings about themselves.

Warning signs:

This is definitely one of the most important sections of the chapter because now we know that child suicide is very real, what are the warning signs to watch out for?

As we saw earlier in the book, there are a lot of warning signs in adults and thankfully the external signs of suicidal ideation in children are similar to the ones that adults might display. But this may vary depending on the child's age, personality and maturity level.

So here are some of the warning signs.

Firstly, changes in behaviours are a sign. For example, if a child suddenly finds it difficult at school, if they withdraw from normal activities, hobbies and friends (like depressed people do) then they become suddenly isolated. As well as their recklessness or impulsivity might increase. In older children and teenagers, their reckless behaviour may include substance use, dangerous driving or sexual promiscuity.

Secondly, if a child excessively talks about dying, self-harm or "going away". Now this a slightly more tricky one because no one shouldn't panic whenever a child brings up death because of course they're going to be curious about this topic. But the danger comes if there is a large focus on it because this could indicate a deeper issue or difficulty. As well as it is important to remember that children, and this is even more so for young children, don't always have words to express that they want to hurt themselves.

Thirdly, changes in a child's mood is a warning sign. For example, if they're appearing excessively sad, anxious, rageful, restless and irritable. All these could be signals that a child struggling with severe mental health or emotional challenges.

In addition, if they have changes in their appetite, sleep patterns or energy levels. These could be a sign of a medical problem so this isn't too dangerous by itself but is when this is combined with other warning signs that this could be indicative of suicidal thoughts or other mental health difficulties.

Overall, the entire point of talking about warning signs is to highlight that many children and adults tip off their caregiver or other loved ones some way about their intentions. They may do it directly but saying something like *I want to die*. Or they may do it indirectly. For example, by saying *nothing matters anymore*, they're moody or recklessly behave.

And in another vein of this indirect tipping off, in some cases children or teenagers don't want to overtly signal what they're thinking, because they could be a shamed or concerned about what their parents will think.

That's why it's important for parents to take other warning signs of mental health seriously and not assume a child's low mood is "just a phase". And again, evidence clearly shows that asking a child or an adolescent about it will not put that idea in their head, if it wasn't already there.

Additionally, and I need to make sure everyone (including me) remembers this, but in the vast majority of cases the children and adolescents want someone to reach out and show them they're loved, supported and more despite the negative pull of their thoughts.

Therefore, stay involved in their academic lives. I'm horrified personally when I hear that parents aren't involved in their child's academic lives, because if they're struggling or need help, how will they know?

And if a parent's kids are still in school then make sure to attend events that are relevant to them. Such as dance performances and sports matches, as well as if there are any academic problems talk to teachers and faculty.

This is all about showing children and adolescents that they aren't alone and that they are so loved and supported.

And if you ever need to talk to your kid about your suspicions, avoid the idea of having "right or wrong" comments and sure the child knows there are no right answers. Instead try to ask open-ended questions (those that are not answered by a simple yes or no), and this will help them open up to you.

Suicide, Young People And University

Moving onto the final section about university, or college as different parts of the world call it, and how this affects young people.

Therefore, when young people are in college, we know this puts a lot of strain on their mental health and we've all heard about the number of university students that commit suicide, so I won't rehash the findings there.

However, when a young person, loved one or friend goes to university, which tends to be outside of their home state, home town or home-whatever, make sure you keep in touch. Let them know how much you're there for them.

Will they get annoyed at you checking in on them maybe once, twice a week?

Maybe they'll say it, and they will say it if you do it *too frequently*. But they won't truly mean it, and it is always better to be slightly annoying with your love, then not, and find out how badly a person you love is struggling so badly with mental health.

This is even more important for freshmen to Americans, first years to the rest of the world, because many of these students are going through many adaptations, so they need to feel that their family support is still there.

Also when you're calling or seeing them to check up on them and how they are, make sure you actually listen. Due to instead of them seeking advice, what many young people need is to be heard. Since young people usually make it clear when they want your objective guidance. So a good approach here is to relate their problems to similar ones that you have had in the past.

And this is a lot better and definitely less intrusive than saying things like, *"I think you should."* If they wanted to hear things like that then they would have asked it differently and telling them what you think they should do isn't exactly the perfect support they probably want.

Instead try to give them the space to figure out what is best for them, discuss the different possibilities as well as show them an angle they might not have considered. That's definitely a great way to show them how much you support them.

And because we're nearing the end of a very long but fascinating chapter, please remember that sometimes children and adolescents don't tell you that they're contemplating suicide because they're worried about how you'll react.

As a result, by using direct, non-judgmental questions that are open-ended you can encourage them to share their thoughts and feelings, and regardless of their response, if you suspect that a person might be suicidal, search for professional help immediately.

Overall, finding out someone you loved is naturally very overwhelming and hopefully you won't have to find that out, and you also tend to question they you're a failure of a parent and more. But just remember that these feelings aren't based in reality in the slightest, but they are understandable. As well as parents never have to navigate their emotions alone.

And this is something we haven't really spoke about in the book until now, but whilst your child gets professional help, make sure you get help too. From seeking the support of family members, friends, a therapist or other confidantes, could all help to ensure that the parent is able to care for themselves while ensuring that their child gets the professional help they need.

WHAT IS SUICIDE GRIEF?

After the difficult topic of the last chapter, I really wanted to focus on something slightly different in this next chapter. So we're going to be focusing on the grief experienced by people who have lost loved ones due to suicide.

This chapter sort of serves two purposes in a way. Firstly, it helps us all to understand what these people sadly have to go through and it offers some unofficial guidance to them. Secondly, in case this has happened to you, this chapter offers some perspective that might help you and it helps you to know that you aren't alone.

Therefore, the death of a loved one, even more so when it comes to suicide has a significant impact on every aspect of their life, from their daily functioning to the home life to work life. They are most likely to have intense feelings of sadness, guilt, confusion, anger and grief.

Of course, there is absolutely no right way for

suicide survivors to grieve or process their feelings or how they feel about everything.

Especially when they have to do a lot of things they never ever thought they would have to. For instance, having to bury their loved ones, take care of finances and the assets the suicide victim left behind and they are struggling with unanswered questions a lot. All of this takes a massive immense toll on the grieving process.

They have to deal with unanswered questions like:

- Why did they do it?
- Is it my fault?
- Were there warning signs I missed?
- How long was my loved one suffering?
- Could I have prevented this?

All I can say here is as we've seen throughout the book, no it wasn't their fault in the slightest, and there's nothing you could have done.

One of the purposes of this book is to teach and help people become more aware of the signs of suicide for the future. But if you don't know this stuff, you simply don't know. No one talks about this so there's no way you could have known the warning signs or done anything.

This isn't your fault.

In addition, when a suicide survivor engages in emotional numbness, this is a very unhealthy coping mechanism done by their mind to avoid the overwhelming and intense emotions like grief. When they engage in emotional numbness and become emotionally numb, they lose the ability to feel and experience their emotions psychologically and emotionally.

This is often done in clinical terms in connection with dissociation and disconnecting from a person's environment, body, feelings, memories and identity.

Suicide survivors feel like their life is upside down, they're struggling to grasp their new reality without their loved one and they are most likely to blame as well as question themselves.

However, it is so critical, as many therapists encourage, that suicide survivors do actually grieve in their own way and seriously process what they're feeling, or their mental health will only get worse over time.

Furthermore, grief from suicide comes in intense waves and it can come with unexpected emotions during the most unpredicted times.

Nevertheless, it is just essential to be patient and kind to yourself and make sure you allow yourself to feel an emotion as it washes through you then it passes.

Then make sure you also embrace the short moments of peace and joy in-between.

Also, don't let your loved one's suicide define them, because it doesn't. Focus on their achievements and they most probably had an incredible life filled with meaning, focus on that joy and celebrate their life.

Moreover, find suicide support groups, because there are so many people like you that are willing to share their own experiences and even if you don't feel ready to share your own just yet, just listen. And know you aren't alone and it will help you to feel less isolated.

Another piece of unofficial advice is to keep a journal because research shows that writing can be a therapeutic way to work through the dark side of grief.

Of course, you will need to be prepared for painful reminders of your loss. For example, holidays you might have booked together but aren't able to go on now, or family holidays like Christmas or whatever else you celebrate. Then there are birthdays and anniversaries as well. In this most impossible of moments, try to celebrate them in honour of your loved one or create new memories on these days by starting new traditions.

In addition, you will have to expect to have ups and downs in the future, so you need to brace yourself for these powerful emotions because you will have some bad days and some good days. Lean into both of them and allow yourself to sit with emotions until they pass.

However, one of the most important things in this entire chapter is you have to allow yourself to find joy. I know many survivors feel guilty about experiencing happiness, but you have to allow yourself to feel joy, to laugh and to have fun. Laughter and joy are not signs of "less grief". Instead they are part of the grieving process and of course your loved one would want you to experience happy moments.

Overall, when you're faced with grief, allow these feelings to flow through you, speak about your grief so it doesn't build up, allow yourself to express your feelings and focus on moving away from the feelings of dying and death towards a focus that promotes life and living.

This entire process and course of both good and bad emotions is normal, okay and part of the grieving process. You can still remember and celebrate your amazing loved one, and still live a purposeful as well as fulfilling life that is not primarily led or ruled by grief.

NEUROPSYCHOLOGY OF SUICIDE

After focusing so much on the social and cognitive factors in the form of mental health conditions that impact people's suicide risk, we now need to really change it up and focus on the biological side of suicide in the form of neuropsychology.

In other words, how does the brain impact a person's chances of committing suicide?

The main reason we're looking at this area is because I truly want to give us all the most information as possible about suicide, and that involves looking at every area possible. Resulting in us now moving onto the brain.

Therefore, to investigate how the brain affects suicide Schmaal et al. (2020) decided to investigate what brain areas were involved in suicidal decision-making, and their results showed that it was the brain areas and systems related to emotion and impulse regulation.

For example, the Ventral Pre-Frontal Cortex

(VPFC) was one of the areas involved with increased suicide risk being associated with impairments in middle as well as side regions of the VPFC, and impairments to the brain connections in this cortex appearing to play a role in excessive negative and blunted positive internal states that can stimulate suicidal ideation.

Additionally, the impairments in the Dorsal Prefrontal Cortex (DPFC) and its connections with the inferior frontal gyrus are associated with suicide attempt behaviours.

Moreover, both the VPFC and DPFC are connected to a portion of the Dorsal Anterior Cingulate Cortez (dACC) and insula. These two brain regions might mediate the transition from suicidal thoughts (as in thinking about suicide) to behaviours (preparing and planning to carry it out and then the suicide itself) by switching between VPFC and DPFC brain systems.

If we connect this information to the other areas of the book, we know from studies like Yeh et al. (2019) that there is a high risk of suicidality amongst clients with depressive disorders, bipolar disorder and schizophrenia spectrum disorders. But if we connect this to neuropsychology then it's interesting to know that these conditions are associated with alterations in the VPFC, insula, dACC and DPFC.

On the whole, there is hope within the neuroscience and psychology communities that if we understand the neurocircuitry well enough in relation to suicide. Then we can hopefully create more effective and targeted interventions and develop more preventive measures.

Before I give a closing remark in this shorter chapter, I want to mention and slightly remind the need for a holistic approach here, because as always it is all well and good us focusing on brain areas, and "fixing" the brain areas to prevent suicide. But it is useless if the person still has social and cognitive factors that make them suicidal.

For example, if they have an unhealthy family dynamic that makes them want to commit suicide, or if they have a negative cognitive style that again makes them see suicide as they only escape, "fixing" brain areas will only go so far.

Therefore, yes we need the neuropsychological interventions for these brain areas but we mustn't forget the importance of psychological treatments too, and even drug interventions if they are absolutely necessary.

But even if that doesn't come completely true, it still connects with what we looked at in chapter two of the book. Due to at the very least all this research proves that there is something more going on behind the cause of suicidal thoughts and behaviours than so-called cowardice, weakness or any number of mistakenly labelled character flaws attributed to those that commit suicide.

WHAT LINKS PERSONALITY AND SUICIDE?

Moving onto personality psychology factors, I want to give you a mini-crash course as a little introduction to personality psychology in case you aren't familiar with it.

The focus of this chapter will be the Big Five Factor Model which divides personality traits into five large categories or factors, and to help you understand this better, below is the extract from my Personality Psychology And Individual Differences book:

"As a result, the Big Five personality factors are:

- Neuroticism
- Extroversion
- Openness to Experience
- Agreeableness
- Conscientiousness

Now, we'll look at these personality factors and all of the information here comes from Pervin et al (2005).

Neuroticism:

This first personality factor assesses a person's maladjustment vs emotional stability. Meaning it finds out if people are prone to unrealistic ideas, psychological distress and excessive cravings or urges. As well as if they have any maladaptive coping responses.

Extroversion

I think we can all agree with has to be the most famous personality factor because of its popularity in media, TV and books. And you can easily see this trait in everyday life.

In addition, this Big factor assesses the quantity and intensity of a person's capacity of joy, interpersonal relationships, activity level and need for simulation.

Since an extrovert has a high activity level with a lot of need for stimulation whereas an introvert is the opposite.

Openness to Experience

This I think has to be one of the most interesting as it looks at a person's behaviour towards proactively seeking out as well as appreciating an experience for their own sake. And it assesses a person's tolerance for exploring the unfamiliar.

Personally, I do like this personality dimension as I think I'm rather high in it because I love exploring new places, the woods and local areas. But to some extent, I don't really like leaving my comfort zone too often depending on the situation.

Agreeableness

Despite the name suggesting you agree with everyone if you're high in this dimension.

Agreeableness looks at how kind, gentle and sympathetic a person is.

Conscientiousness:

The last dimension assesses an individual's degree of organisation, persistence and motivation in goal directed behaviour. As well as it contrasts people who are dependable and organised with people who are lackadaisical and sloppy."

Personality and Suicide:

Now we know the basics of personality psychology, the Big Five factor model has been found to predict a wide range of important life outcomes. For instance, after general intelligence, conscientiousness is the single best predictor of a person's work or academic performance.

Also, as you'll see in the next chapter, it has long been known that personality disorders, like Borderline Personality Disorder, are associated with higher risk of suicide. Yet it is less well known that 5% of Antisocial Personality Disorder will eventually die by suicide.

For the next part of the chapter, we're going to be looking at a range of research behind personality factors and suicide, then I'll explain the implications of the results at the end.

Firstly, Ansell et al. (2015) investigated 431 patients with personality disorders for 10 years, and over that time 13.5% of the patients made at least one or more suicide attempts with the maximum being 11. Therefore, showing that people with personality disorders are at a higher risk of suicide compared to the general population.

Secondly, other researchers wanted to investigate the relationship between a person's suicide risk and the five-factor personality traits. For instance, Duberstein et al. (2000) examined 81 depressed inpatients who were aged 50 or over, and the researchers found they had higher levels of neuroticism and openness to experience. Both of these were associated with having a history of suicidal ideation, whereas lower levels of extraversion was associated with having a history of past suicide attempts.

Thirdly, within the same research vein as Duberstein, McCann (2010) looked at the relationship of personality at a State level in the US (for example people in Nebraska are less neurotic than people in New Jersey) and compared it to the state's suicide completion rates. The results showed that higher neuroticism rates in states and lower levels of agreeableness increased rates of death by suicide. Those two personality traits combined accounted for approximately half of the variance in suicide rates amongst all 50 states.

Then if we move onto studies that had much larger sample sizes, Bluml et al. (2013) looked at 2,555 German citizens and assessed their Big Five personality traits and suicide risk. Bluml's results found significant differences between men and women. Such as female suicide risk was increased when neuroticism was higher and when openness to experience was higher. Whereas male suicide risk decreased in the presence of higher extroversion and higher conscientiousness.

I'll talk about the results in a moment.

For our penultimate study, Soltaninejad et al. (2014) studied 1,659 members of the Iranian armed forces. This is great on its own because it allows the literature to have a wide range of findings from different countries and cultures to inform their results, so we can predict or suggest a universal rule of behaviour which personality factors for suicide seems to be.

Therefore, their results found neuroticism was a stronger predictor of current suicidal thinking, then extroversion was the second, and then agreeableness was the third. Meaning that higher levels of neuroticism, lower extroversion and agreeableness increased risk of suicidal ideation in this sample.

Finally, the largest study that I could find was Batty et al. (2018) who monitored 464,251 participants in several countries over a period of 8 years. During this time 270 participants died by suicide, and the results found higher levels of neuroticism significantly increased suicide risk and lower levels of agreeableness contributed to higher risk as well but less dramatically.

Discussion Of Results

In terms of the results, some researchers have dubbed these findings as the "Misery Triad". Due to the combination of these traits suggests the person has a greater sensitivity to emotional pain, they lack effectiveness in solving their difficulties and resisting impulses and a deficiency of social support. Also, studies that implicated lower agreeableness added to "lack of social support increases suicide risk" hypothesis.

Overall, neuroticism is clearly a strong factor when it comes to suicide risk and it should be corrected by psychotherapy that this teaches the person how to better manage negative emotions and in some cases psychiatric medication might be appropriate too in the intervention.

For the lower conscientiousness risk factor, this is a risk factor because these people are more impulsive and might be more at risk of making poorly considered decisions to attempt suicide. As well as it is associated with worse performance in school and at work. This is very important to remember as a third of successful suicides are unemployed at time of death.

But one personality trait that does need more research into is the openness to experience, because suicide isn't the sort of open experience that people should want to experience, and this is a surprising finding that researchers don't understand.

Yet.

OTHER MENTAL HEALTH
CONDITIONS AND SUICIDE

To sort of start wrapping up the book, these final two chapters are going to be picking up on details that we might have missed in other chapters. For example, in this chapter because we have already spoken about depression and bipolar disorder a lot in the book, we now need to focus on some other mental health conditions to see how they impact suicide.

Suicide Amongst Post-Traumatic Stress Disorder

The first condition we'll look at is PTSD and this develops in the aftermath of a traumatic event, with it being a complex condition that manifests in several different ways. Including, depression, dissociation and anxiety. Leading PTSD to reduce a person's quality of life and it is sometimes implicated in suicide.

Additionally, according to a September 2018 VA report, the veterans overall suicide rate is approximately 1.5 times higher than non-veterans, with male veterans more likely than females.

Saying that, in the last few years, suicides amongst female veterans have been rapidly increasing with recent evidence suggesting female veterans are more likely by two to five times to die by suicide compared to non-veteran females.

Overall, if someone has PTSD then it is critical that they seek professional help for the condition. Not only so they can improve their quality of life, but so they can also prevent possible suicide down the line.

Borderline Personality Disorder

The second condition we'll be looking at is Borderline Personality Disorder with it being characterised by a person's unstable moods, intense fear of abandonment as well as difficulty in maintaining personal relationships.

In terms of suicide, this is an important condition to look at because approximately 70% of people with Borderline Personality Disorder will attempt suicide, 10% will die by it.

The treatment for the condition is typically a form of psychotherapy, like Dialectical behavioural therapy, that is combined with medication, leaving people able to be stabilised and live fulfilling productive lives.

Moreover, if we cast our minds back to the second chapter of the book on myths and the reference to *suicide as attention seeking,* this is slightly possible with Borderline Personality Disorder as threats of suicide or self-harm are a common symptom of BPD especially in response to perceived rejection or abandonment by friends, loved ones or romantic partners. Yet it is still important that threats are be taken seriously as many people BPD do attempt it.

On the other hand, these threats of suicide do create intense emotional strain or frustration for the people on the receiving end, even more when it occurs often over a long period of time, so anyone who thinks a loved one at risk should help immediately.

I'll fully admit this is a trickier condition to work with because the use of suicide threats is common, but considering how many BPD sufferers do attempt suicide, getting professional help is still just as critical as it is for any other case.

Substance Abuse and Suicide

The penultimate condition we need to focus on is substance abuse and this is a very important one to look at because it of how common it is. Especially with substance abusers being approximately 6 times more likely to die by suicide than the general population.

Also it's good to note that many people with addiction who consider suicide do struggle with depression or another mental health condition. This only increases the risk of suicide anyway.

Therefore, the best way to avoid a suicide is to treat the addiction and any other concurrent condition at the same time to decrease the risk of suicide and help the person better cope with negative emotions in the future.

As well as one of the reasons why substance abuse is a flawed maladaptive coping mechanism is because drug use itself can trigger depressive states or low mood, as seen in "downer" drugs like alcohol or sedatives. Then other kinds of drugs lower inhibitions, leading people to behave impulsively or take dangerous actions they wouldn't take while sober.

And referring to the coping mechanism, drug use could attempt to cope with negative emotions, it actually may help suppress bad feelings in the short term. But that's the thing about the short term, it's short and drugs tends to worsen a person's emotional state over time, and when drugs run out and painful emotions come back, the person could feel overwhelmed by sadness and consider suicide a way out.

Attention-Deficit Hyperactivity Disorder, Autism and Suicide

In the stages of writing this book, there was actually going to be a chapter dedicated to this condition because I found a rather interesting looking article that I was going to save for later. Yet when I came back to the article, I realised the single research study mentioned in it was far too tedious for my liking, so I ditched the idea.

Thankfully, I managed to find a new study that

helps to examine how ADHD and suicide interconnect in the form of Furczyk et al. (2014) and a few others in the reference section at the end of the book.

The study shows that ADHD appears to cause a noticeable increased risk of suicide, because people with the condition struggle with impulsivity, so they could be more likely to engage in self-harming behaviour or consider suicide when faced with a career setback, low mood or relationship upset.

Furthermore, impulsive people are more likely to take part in substance abuse. This as we saw in the last section can increase the risk of suicide.

Also, the symptoms of inattention may lead to the person experiencing social, career or academic-related challenges which results in damage to their self-esteem, as well as persistently low self-esteem or feelings that they're a failure can trigger or worsen suicidal ideation.

Additionally, ADHD and depression frequently appear side by side and this further heightens the risk of suicidal thoughts or behaviour.

Similarly, evidence from Hirvikoski et al. (2020) suggests that people with Autism Spectrum Conditions are significantly more likely to attempt suicide than the general population, with them being approximately 4 to 6 times more likely. The risk appears to be even greater for women with autism and that is probably linked to the diagnostic and support problems engrained in ASC towards women, but that's beyond the scope of this book.

As well as people who also have ADHD or have ADHD and an intellectual disability are maybe at an even greater risk according to Hirvikoski et al. (2020).

Overall, the data suggests clinicians should be especially vigilant for signs of suicidality in individuals with autism and experts argue particularly if other risk factors are present.

And to finish up this mental health section of the book, I just wanted to jump in here and remind us of all, including myself, that yes having a mental health condition does affect a person's quality of life, causes psychological distress and results in maladaptive coping mechanisms that need to be effectively trained out of a person.

It does not mean they are "fated" (if you believe in that stuff) to commit suicide or attempt it.

I know a lot of the book has focused on mental health conditions and how they impact suicide, but the former does not guarantee the latter.

My point is if you know someone who has a mental health condition that we're spoken about in the book, please don't panic that they're "doomed" to attempt suicide. They aren't.

Just love them, support them and if they show a warning sign or you're concerned about them, then take action and make sure they know how much you value them.

OTHER SUICIDE RISK FACTORS

For the final chapter of the book, I know we've covered a lot of suicide risk factors and why people might unfortunately choose suicide as the only way to stop the pain. But suicide isn't always down or caused by mental health conditions, substance abuse or any other conditions.

Instead, the person's choice could be down to one or more wide ranging sociocultural or physical factors. For example, chronic pain, job loss, unemployment or serious legal trouble (as we saw in the prison chapter) and genetics. As well as I'm sure you've noticed through the book, but suicide is a very complicated matter.

Therefore, there are a few more causes or risk factors we need to look at together before we finish up our psychology journey.

Economic And Social Challenges:

As social and other fields of psychology teaches us, as a species as humans do not exist in a vacuum.

We are constantly influenced by external and internal factors from our social groups to our biology to our society.

As humans, we are very, very dependent on other people and communities for resources, social contact, food and nourishment (sustenance) and endless other needs.

As a result, when these connections are severed for whatever reason, the effect of this is very severe, and sometimes drive others to suicide.

In terms of economic factors, if someone has lost their job then this creates significant financial challenges for them that are hard to overcome. The social and economic factors themselves worsen a person's risk of suicide, but being evicted and unable to pay rent is strongly associated with increased risk of suicidal thoughts and behaviours.

Additionally, there is evidence that 1 in 3 people who died by suicide were unemployed at the time. As well as during economic downturns, there's an increase in suicide rates. For example, evidence from the 2008 recession showed that there was an associated 13% increase in suicides, with many of these being attributed to unemployment.

In terms of genetics and I realise this is a bit off the cuff, but because mental health conditions have a genetic component and the certain conditions themselves can increase the risk of suicide. There's an argument too that genetics are a suicide risk factor, but of course it is a lot more complicated than that.

That's why it's a bit off the cuff without me going into too much depth.

How Chronic Pain Links With Suicide?

This was definitely a bit of a surprise for me to learn about because I never would have considered this a risk factor, but of course now I know about it, it makes perfect sense.

Chronic pain increases the risk of suicide too because evidence suggests that chronic pain sufferers are twice as likely to consider suicide. This is even more true if they suffer long term severe pain, and this can significantly interfere with a person's ability to work, take care of themselves and provide for a family.

Resulting in feelings of inadequacy, it can strain their relationships and put financial challenges on them, and then to make this even worse this is combined with the daily agony of the pain itself. Leading to significantly worsen a person's mental health over a period of months or years.

This is absolutely terrible, but sadly the bad news doesn't always stop here.

Since if the cause of the chronic pain is unclear or their treatment is ineffective, then this can and does lead to feelings of hopelessness. And that same happens if a person's chronic pain is dismissed or ignored by doctors. All resulting in a person's well-being being damaged further, and suicide being seen as the only way out.

And even some of the medication given to

people with chronic pain isn't great, because opioid medication is frequently prescribed to treat chronic pain. But it can lead to mental or physical dependence on the drug so when the medication runs out or is otherwise no longer available, the withdrawal symptoms can heighten their feelings of despair.

Thankfully, there are things that can be done about chronic pain and decrease the suicidal feelings. Like having effective medical treatment reduces or eliminates chronic pain, leading to a significantly lower suicide risk.

Equally, if the biological treatments are imperfect then psychological treatments, like mindfulness-based stress based or Cognitive Behavioural Therapy or lifestyle changes promoting a healthier diet, better sleep and physical activity can all help build up a person's self-efficacy, as well as target their rumination and anxiety that are inherent to chronic pain.

Overall, with their mental health improving because of the effective treatment, and they no longer have the rumination as well as the anxiety surrounding their chronic pain, this all leads to a reduction of the intensity and frequency of their suicidal behaviours and thoughts.

And that's a great result for anyone.

CONCLUSION

After looking at the causes, risk factors, how to prevent suicide and more, we need to wrap up everything, and this is definitely easier said than done. Simply because we have looked at so much, so instead I will just give some unofficial pointers and tips for all of us moving forward.

Thankfully, many of us will never have to deal with suicide directly, and for the people who picked up this book because they were curious about learning more about suicide. It is great that you have wanted to learn more and now you know that there are so many myths and harming misconceptions about suicide, and now all of us know what actually happens.

Therefore, to these people, I, of course, thank you massively for picking up this book, and I think going forward we just need to challenge people when they repeat the false damaging myths that only harm suicidal individuals instead of helping them.

Because let's face it, these myths kill people. These myths stop people from feeling able to reach out and get support, so these myths need to end. And that can all start with us challenging them whenever we face them.

For the people who have faced loss by suicide and you picked up this book, I know you will probably be in the minority of the readers. But I really hope I gave you something useful. Maybe I helped you understand what happened, maybe I helped you understand that it wasn't your fault and maybe I helped give you a little bit of closure.

And like all readers of my books, it's been a privilege that you picked up my book on the topic.

Just remember that no suicide is your fault and now we all know about the warning signs, the causes and the research about suicide. We can all watch our loved ones just in case this happens, because it is always better to know than not know, and then something bad happens.

Finally, I have no idea if anyone who is thinking about suicide would read a book like this, but just in case they are. Please just get professional help, talk to someone and just know that you are loved, supported and cherished by your loved ones.

You might be feeling alone right now and like you are an awful burden on the entire world. I know that, truly. But things do get so much better and you really are loved.

We have explored in the book how to tell others

about your feelings, the importance of hotlines and what to do if you cannot talk to your loved ones. But seek help, you aren't worthless and the world does need you, no matter what your thoughts tell you otherwise.

I truly hope that everyone has gotten something out of this book. Personally I loved writing it and I truly hope that this helps to make a difference to someone's life.

I doubt I will, I really do, but I had to try.

REFERENCE LIST

Alcaide, J., Guirado, R., Crespo, C. et al. (2019). Alterations of perineuronal nets in the dorsolateral prefrontal cortex of neuropsychiatric patients. Int. J. Bipolar Disord., 7:24. doi.org/10.1186/s40345-019-0161-0

Ansell, E. B., Wright, A. G., Markowitz, J. C., Sanislow, C. A., Hopwood, C. J., Zanarini, M. C., ... & Grilo, C. M. (2015). Personality disorder risk factors for suicide attempts over 10 years of follow-up. *Personality Disorders: Theory, Research, and Treatment*, *6*(2), 161.

Asarnow JR & Mehlum L. (2019). Practitioner Review: Treatment for suicidal and self-harming adolescents - advances in suicide prevention care. Journal of child psychology and psychiatry, and allied disciplines, 60(10), 1046–1054. https://doi.org/10.1111/jcpp.13130

Batty, G. D., Gale, C. R., Tanji, F., Gunnell, D., Kivimäki, M., Tsuji, I., & Jokela, M. (2018).

Personality traits and risk of suicide mortality: findings from a multi-cohort study in the general population. *World psychiatry : official journal of the World Psychiatric Association (WPA)*, *17*(3), 371–372. https://doi.org/10.1002/wps.20575

Bouras C., Kövari E., Hof P.R., et al. (2001). Anterior cingulate cortex pathology in schizophrenia and bipolar disorder. Acta Neuropathol., 102(4):373-9. 10.1007/s004010100392

Bridge, J. A., Asti, L., Horowitz, L. M., Greenhouse, J. B., Fontanella, C. A., Sheftall, A. H., ... & Campo, J. V. (2015). Suicide trends among elementary school–aged children in the United States from 1993 to 2012. *JAMA pediatrics*, *169*(7), 673-677.

Curtin, S. C., & Heron, M. P. (2019). Death rates due to suicide and homicide among persons aged 10–24: United States, 2000–2017.

Duberstein, P. R., Conwell, Y., Seidlitz, L., Denning, D. G., Cox, C., & Caine, E. D. (2000). Personality traits and suicidal behavior and ideation in depressed inpatients 50 years of age and older. *The journals of gerontology. Series B, Psychological sciences and social sciences*, *55*(1), P18–P26. https://doi.org/10.1093/geronb/55.1.p18

Duncan, D.T. and Hatzenbuehler, M.L., 2014. Lesbian, gay, bisexual, and transgender hate crimes and suicidality among a population-based sample of sexual-minority adolescents in Boston. American journal of public health, 104(2), pp.272-278.

Furczyk K & Thome J. (2014). Adult ADHD and suicide. Atten Defic Hyperact Disord. 6(3):153-8.

Gunnell D, Appleby L, Arensman E, et al. (2020). Suicide risk and prevention during the COVID-19 pandemic. Lancet Psychiatry. 7(6):468-471. doi:10.1016/S2215-0366(20)30171-1

Hirvikoski, T., Boman, M., Chen, Q., D'Onofrio, B., Mittendorfer-Rutz, E., Lichtenstein, P., . . . Larsson, H. (n.d.). (2020) Individual risk and familial liability for suicide attempt and suicide in autism: A population-based study. Psychological Medicine, 1-12. doi:10.1017/S0033291719001405

https://archive.nytimes.com/newoldage.blogs.nytimes.com/2013/08/07/high-suicide-rates-among-the-elderly

https://www.canada.ca/en/public-health/services/publications/healthy-living/suicide-canada-key-statistics-infographic.html

https://www.nimh.nih.gov/health/statistics/suicide

https://www.psychologytoday.com/gb/basics/depression/depression-and-suicide

https://www.psychologytoday.com/gb/basics/suicide/how-talk-about-suicidal-thoughts

https://www.psychologytoday.com/gb/basics/suicide/warning-signs-suicide

https://www.psychologytoday.com/gb/blog/cell-block/201902/suicide-behind-bars

https://www.psychologytoday.com/gb/blog/happiness-is-state-mind/202109/suicide-prevention-awareness-month-what-is-suicide-grief

https://www.psychologytoday.com/gb/blog/reading-between-the-headlines/201412/suicide-and-the-holidays

https://www.psychologytoday.com/us/blog/happiness-is-state-mind/202005/mental-health-and-job-loss

https://www.psychologytoday.com/us/blog/nation-in-pain/201511/chronic-pain-and-the-risk-suicide

https://www.psychologytoday.com/us/blog/talking-about-men/202109/the-silent-crisis-male-suicide

https://www.psychologytoday.com/us/blog/talking-about-men/202109/the-silent-crisis-male-suicide

https://www.spectrumnews.org/news/autistic-women-twice-as-likely-as-autistic-men-to-attempt-suicide/

Impey M & Heun R. (2012) Completed suicide, ideation and attempt in attention deficit hyperactivity disorder. Acta Psychiatr Scand. 125(2):93-102.

Isumi A, Doi S, Yamaoka Y, Takahashi K, Fujiwara T. (2020). Do suicide rates in children and adolescents change during school closure in Japan? The acute effect of the first wave of COVID-19 pandemic on child and adolescent mental health [published online ahead of print, 2020 Aug 23]. Child Abuse Negl. doi:10.1016/j.chiabu.2020.104680

Ivey-Stephenson, A. Z., Demissie, Z., Crosby, A. E.,

Stone, D. M., Gaylor, E., Wilkins, N., ... & Brown, M. (2020). Suicidal ideation and behaviors among high school students—youth risk behavior survey, United States, 2019. *MMWR supplements*, *69*(1), 47.

Janiri, D., Doucet, G. E., Pompili, M., Sani, G., Luna, B., Brent, D. A., & Frangou, S. (2020). Risk and protective factors for childhood suicidality: a US population-based study. *The Lancet Psychiatry*, *7*(4), 317-326.

Killgore WDS, Cloonan SA, Taylor EC, et al. (2020). Trends in suicidal ideation over the first three months of COVID-19 lockdowns [published online ahead of print, 2020 Aug 17]. Psychiatry Res. 293:113390. doi:10.1016/j.psychres.2020.113390

McCann S. J. (2010). Suicide, big five personality factors, and depression at the American state level. *Archives of suicide research : official journal of the International Academy for Suicide Research*, *14*(4), 368–374. https://doi.org/10.1080/13811118.2010.524070

Namkung, H., Kim, S. H., & Sawa, A. (2017). The Insula: An Underestimated Brain Area in Clinical Neuroscience, Psychiatry, and Neurology. Trends in Neurosciences, 40(4):200–207. https://doi.org/10.1016/j.tins.2017.02.002

Nordentoft M & Erlangsen A. (2019). Suicide-turning the tide. Science (New York, N.Y.), 365(6455), 725. https://doi.org/10.1126/science.aaz1568

Schmaal, L., van Harmelen, A.L., Chatzi, V. et al. (2020). Imaging suicidal thoughts and behaviors: a comprehensive review of 2 decades of neuroimaging studies. Mol. Psychiatry, 25:408–427. doi.org/10.1038/s41380-019-0587-x

Soltaninejad, A., Fathi-Ashtiani, A., Ahmadi, K., Mirsharafoddini, H. S., Nikmorad, A., & Pilevarzadeh, M. (2014). Personality factors underlying suicidal behavior among military youth. *Iranian Red Crescent medical journal*, *16*(4), e12686. https://doi.org/10.5812/ircmj.12686

Turecki G & Brent DA (2016). Suicide and suicidal behaviour. The Lancet, 387, 1227–1239.

Twenge JM, Joiner TE. (2020). U.S. Census Bureau-assessed prevalence of anxiety and depressive symptoms in 2019 and during the 2020 COVID-19 pandemic [published online ahead of print, 2020 Jul 15]. Depress Anxiety. 10.1002/da.23077. doi:10.1002/da.23077

Uddin R, Burton NW, Maple M, Khan SR, Khan A. (2019). Suicidal ideation, suicide planning, and suicide attempts among adolescents in 59 low-income and middle-income countries: a population-based study. The Lancet Child & Adolescent Health. 3 (4): 223–233. doi:10.1016/S2352-4642(18)30403-6. PMID 30878117.

VA National Suicide Data Report 2005-2016, Office of Mental Health and Suicide Prevention, September 2018

Womer, F. Y., Kalmar, J. H., Wang, F., & Blumberg, H. P. (2009). A Ventral Prefrontal-Amygdala Neural System in Bipolar Disorder: A View from Neuroimaging Research. Acta Neuropsychiatrica, 21(6):228–238. PMCID: PMC2911239

Yeh, H. H., Westphal, J., Hu, Y. et al. (2019). Diagnosed mental health conditions and risk of suicide mortality. Psychiatric Services, 70(9):750–757. doi: 10.1176/appi.ps.201800346

CHECK OUT THE PSYCHOLOGY WORLD PODCAST FOR MORE PSYCHOLOGY INFORMATION! AVAILABLE ON ALL MAJOR PODCAST APPS.

About the author:

Connor Whiteley is the author of over 60 books in the sci-fi fantasy, nonfiction psychology and books for writer's genre and he is a Human Branding Speaker and Consultant.

He is a passionate warhammer 40,000 reader, psychology student and author.

Who narrates his own audiobooks and he hosts The Psychology World Podcast.

All whilst studying Psychology at the University of Kent, England.

Also, he was a former Explorer Scout where he gave a speech to the Maltese President in August 2018 and he attended Prince Charles' 70th Birthday Party at Buckingham Palace in May 2018.

Plus, he is a self-confessed coffee lover!

OTHER SHORT STORIES BY CONNOR WHITELEY

Mystery Short Stories:

A Smokey Way To Go

A Spicy Way To GO

A Marketing Way To Go

A Missing Way To Go

A Showering Way To Go

Poison In The Candy Cane

Christmas Innocence

You Better Watch Out

Christmas Theft

Trouble In Christmas

Smell of The Lake

Problem In A Car

Theft, Past and Team

Embezzler In The Room

A Strange Way To Go

A Horrible Way To Go

Ann Awful Way To Go

An Old Way To Go

A Fishy Way To Go

A Pointy Way To Go

A High Way To Go

A Fiery Way To Go

A Glassy Way To Go

A Chocolatey Way To Go

Kendra Detective Mystery Collection Volume 1

Kendra Detective Mystery Collection Volume 2

Stealing A Chance At Freedom

Glassblowing and Death

Theft of Independence

Cookie Thief

Marble Thief

Book Thief

Art Thief

Mated At The Morgue

The Big Five Whoopee Moments

Stealing An Election

Mystery Short Story Collection Volume 1

Mystery Short Story Collection Volume 2

Science Fiction Short Stories:

Gummy Bear Detective

The Candy Detective

What Candies Fear

The Blurred Image

Shattered Legions

The First Rememberer

Life of A Rememberer

System of Wonder

Lifesaver

Remarkable Way She Died
The Interrogation of Annabella Stormic
Blade of The Emperor
Arbiter's Truth
Computation of Battle
Old One's Wrath
Puppets and Masters
Ship of Plague
Interrogation
Edge of Failure
One Way Choice
Acceptable Losses
Balance of Power
Good Idea At The Time
Escape Plan
Escape In The Hesitation
Inspiration In Need
Singing Warriors
Knowledge is Power
Killer of Polluters
Climate of Death
The Family Mailing Affair
Defining Criminality
The Martian Affair
A Cheating Affair
The Little Café Affair
Mountain of Death

Prisoner's Fight
Claws of Death
Bitter Air
Honey Hunt
Blade On A Train

<u>Fantasy Short Stories:</u>
City of Snow
City of Light
City of Vengeance
Dragons, Goats and Kingdom
Smog The Pathetic Dragon
Don't Go In The Shed
The Tomato Saver
The Remarkable Way She Died
The Bloodied Rose
Asmodia's Wrath
Heart of A Killer
Emissary of Blood
Dragon Coins
Dragon Tea
Dragon Rider
Sacrifice of the Soul
Heart of The Flesheater
Heart of The Regent
Heart of The Standing
Feline of The Lost

Heart of The Story
City of Fire
Awaiting Death

Other books by Connor Whiteley:
Bettie English Private Eye Series
A Very Private Woman
The Russian Case
A Very Urgent Matter
A Case Most Personal
Trains, Scots and Private Eyes
The Federation Protects

The Fireheart Fantasy Series
Heart of Fire
Heart of Lies
Heart of Prophecy
Heart of Bones
Heart of Fate

City of Assassins (Urban Fantasy)
City of Death
City of Marytrs
City of Pleasure
City of Power

Agents of The Emperor
Return of The Ancient Ones
Vigilance
Angels of Fire
Kingmaker
The Eight
The Lost Generation
Lord Of War Trilogy (Agents of The
Emperor)
Not Scared Of The Dark
Madness
Burn It All Down

The Garro Series- Fantasy/Sci-fi
GARRO: GALAXY'S END
GARRO: RISE OF THE ORDER
GARRO: END TIMES
GARRO: SHORT STORIES
GARRO: COLLECTION
GARRO: HERESY
GARRO: FAITHLESS
GARRO: DESTROYER OF WORLDS
GARRO: COLLECTIONS BOOK 4-6
GARRO: MISTRESS OF BLOOD
GARRO: BEACON OF HOPE
GARRO: END OF DAYS

Winter Series- Fantasy Trilogy Books
WINTER'S COMING
WINTER'S HUNT
WINTER'S REVENGE
WINTER'S DISSENSION

Miscellaneous:
RETURN
FREEDOM
SALVATION
Reflection of Mount Flame
The Masked One
The Great Deer

Gay Romance Novellas
Breaking, Nursing, Repiaring A Broken Heart
Jacob And Daniel
Fallen For A Lie

Companion guides:
BIOLOGICAL PSYCHOLOGY 2ND
EDITION WORKBOOK
COGNITIVE PSYCHOLOGY 2ND
EDITION WORKBOOK
SOCIOCULTURAL PSYCHOLOGY 2ND
EDITION WORKBOOK
ABNORMAL PSYCHOLOGY 2ND

EDITION WORKBOOK
PSYCHOLOGY OF HUMAN
RELATIONSHIPS 2ND EDITION
WORKBOOK
HEALTH PSYCHOLOGY WORKBOOK
FORENSIC PSYCHOLOGY WORKBOOK

Audiobooks by Connor Whiteley:
BIOLOGICAL PSYCHOLOGY
COGNITIVE PSYCHOLOGY
SOCIOCULTURAL PSYCHOLOGY
ABNORMAL PSYCHOLOGY
PSYCHOLOGY OF HUMAN
RELATIONSHIPS
HEALTH PSYCHOLOGY
DEVELOPMENTAL PSYCHOLOGY
RESEARCH IN PSYCHOLOGY
FORENSIC PSYCHOLOGY
GARRO: GALAXY'S END
GARRO: RISE OF THE ORDER
GARRO: SHORT STORIES
GARRO: END TIMES
GARRO: COLLECTION
GARRO: HERESY
GARRO: FAITHLESS
GARRO: DESTROYER OF WORLDS

GARRO: COLLECTION BOOKS 4-6
GARRO: COLLECTION BOOKS 1-6

Business books:
TIME MANAGEMENT: A GUIDE FOR
STUDENTS AND WORKERS
LEADERSHIP: WHAT MAKES A GOOD
LEADER? A GUIDE FOR STUDENTS
AND WORKERS.
BUSINESS SKILLS: HOW TO SURVIVE
THE BUSINESS WORLD? A GUIDE FOR
STUDENTS, EMPLOYEES AND
EMPLOYERS.
BUSINESS COLLECTION

GET YOUR FREE BOOK AT:
WWW.CONNORWHITELEY.NET

CPSIA information can be obtained
at www.ICGtesting.com
Printed in the USA
LVHW081204210223
739960LV00017B/1592

9 781915 551382